THE GREAT GLOBAL
TREASURE HUNT
ON
GOOGLE EARTH

DEDOPULOS

ILLUSTRATED BY JONATHAN LUCAS

CARLTON
BOOKS

THE BEGINNING OF THE END?

I dreamed, and within the dream were such sights and voices as I have never known before. Ancient landscapes and forgotten wonders vied with all manner of beasts and birds, and above them all towered a mighty treasure of gold. When I awoke, I understood the nature of the task that awaited me. I was to build a cunning labyrinth out of the world itself, a test of ingenuity that would reward the dedicated. Seeker, you hold my labyrinth in your hands.

I wish to reassure you that any person may attempt to solve my puzzle. No specific skill is required; no particular expertise or cultural background or age. All you need is an enquiring mind, a careful eye, and the will to seek the solution. Nothing more is necessary. Champion, you are reading my words. I know not your age, sex or nationality, but you are the one above all, one who will win my treasure, earn my admiration.

As you explore this book, you will discover that it consists of a series of images. I have included a commentary with most, but not all. Each image contains a number of clues in various guises. These clues, taken together, will lead you to a solution - perhaps a place, a person, an object or a concept. You may find that the solutions get trickier to discover as you progress through the book, but do not be disheartened. Once you have all 14 solutions, those will form one last puzzle. By considering them with suitable diligence, you will find yourself led to one specific place on the face of Google Earth. That most special of locations is the answer you seek, the heart of my labyrinth, the key that will open the door to the treasure.

There are some things which will be helpful to bear in your mind as you seek solution. The first is a simple warning to be wary; not every detail in each image is a clue. Some elements are merely there for decoration or atmosphere. Such elements may lead you astray, so do exercise judgement. You should also be aware that each clue refers to one aspect of the solution. By looking at the clues from different angles, and considering their implications with respect to each other, you will discover the swiftest path to the solution.

Some clues will guide you towards the solution through their direct associations. A bottle of French champagne, for example, may point towards Reims, the largest city in the Champagne region and one of the centres of champagne production in France. Other clues may be more cryptic, or provide a link to something associated with the solution, rather than to the solution itself. A very few clues might even refer directly to the final answer itself. If there was a clue that was spread over more than one image, it would most certainly be a reference to the final answer. None of the clues are based on linguistic puns however, so you can safely discount that as an avenue of exploration.

In each image, at least one clue will be a direct representation of a place on the face of the planet. This may be the pattern formed by a network of roads or rivers, or an area of landscape, or even the likeness of a specific building or large object. These locations are often useful in finding or confirming their respective solutions. Other clues in the image will lead you to the approximate vicinity of that location.

In order to make sense of these location clues, and discover the final answer, you will need to make use of Google Earth. If you do not yet know of it, it is a complete map of the Earth that you can explore from your computer. Easy to use, it contains satellite photographs of the entire world, combined with map information and Google's powerful search engine. Using it, you can fly to any place on the globe's surface, and zoom out to the view from space, or close in, right down to street level. It is very easy to use, and available for free download from http://earth.google.com - it will run successfully on the vast majority of computers in use that can connect to the internet.

Different location clues will become clear at different heights above ground level. It may take a little searching to locate some of them, so be patient if you cannot place them immediately. In some instances, you may find the location clues easier to place if you select the Google Earth option to display roads; in other instances, it may be clearer without. Various other Google Earth options may also prove useful in some cases.

Linked to this book is a website, www.jointhetreasurehunt.com At various times, I will provide hints, tips, further clues and maybe even a few individual solutions via this website. The website also has space to submit your answer, so you will not be able to win the prize without it.

It will also prove to your benefit to follow my related English-language twitter feed, www.twitter.com/dedopulos, and keep an eye on my other activities on and off the web. It is true to say that when solving any puzzle, the more you know about the mind that created it, the simpler it will be. If you come to understand how I think, you will undoubtedly have an easier time in your quest to claim my treasure.

Once you are confident that you have located the place on the Earth that holds my treasure, you may submit your solution.

Good luck to you, Seeker. You have taken the first step on my quest. Be steadfast. An enthralling journey and wondrous treasure await.

DEDOPULOS

1. FACING THE GALLOWS

As the sun rises, golden light spills over the land. The shadows it casts are long, like fingers. This is how it begins, and suddenly the way before me is clear. At last, I see. There will be long journeys. Strange paths to follow, and stranger tides. Round and round and round again I go.

There was a man - or maybe there was a half-man; wise and fey, he revealed great secrets that shook the very Earth. His counsel will guide me. There have been others too, in their multitudes, from all corners of our world. Some stand beside me now, and shine in the glory of this mightiest day. Only a select few endure, and their voices sigh on the wind.

I, however, will stand. Wonders and mysteries will be my companions, from the circle and from the track. As I gaze into the dawn, I hear a mighty voice cry forth, "Rejoice! The day has come at last, and to the devoted, all will be revealed."

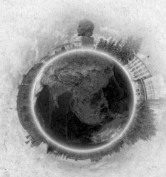

2. GEORGIA ON MY MIND

I find myself sinking through darkness. Around me, I can hear tormented groans and sudden laughter, the clattering of bones, and above all, the horrible sound of bells. Slowly, a heat begins to rise. It builds in the soles of my feet, warmer and warmer, and I find myself remembering distant times.

There was a world of light and laughter, of lamps festooned in the palms like ribbons. The sudden spray of water. Elegant arches, dainty tables, and on my arm a dream of beauty. We talked of Gawain and fishermen, of Pepys and Newton, of the Oldest of the Old. The stars spread their wings over us, and settled across the paving slabs like jewels.

But all times must draw to an end.

All things must pass. The heat rises, reminding me that in the end, even bone must crumble. Ashes to ashes, dust to dust. It is the way of things. With that realisation, the darkness shatters and blows away, spindrift on the breeze.

3. GETTING AHEAD

In the Elder days, before mankind, the Earth had other masters. We were not the first, and we'll not be the last. Before us, Colossi walked where now we tread. They raised their tools and smote the land, carving it to their strange designs. In the sea they dwelled, and the sky, and deep in the roots of mountains, and they bred horrors and marvels alike. When their time came, they did not die, but merely went beyond.

How do you describe that which is outside all points of reference? Say that it is the flavour of deep green, the scent of brass angels, the texture of fear? Some things have no context outside of being experienced. To know the underworld, the place Outside, you must walk its graven passages.

There are wheels within wheels, spinning as they will. Each is unique, vast, unfathomable. When they align, strange aeons will come at last, and then who knows the fate of man? Some things are better left unquestioned.

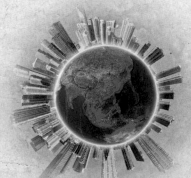

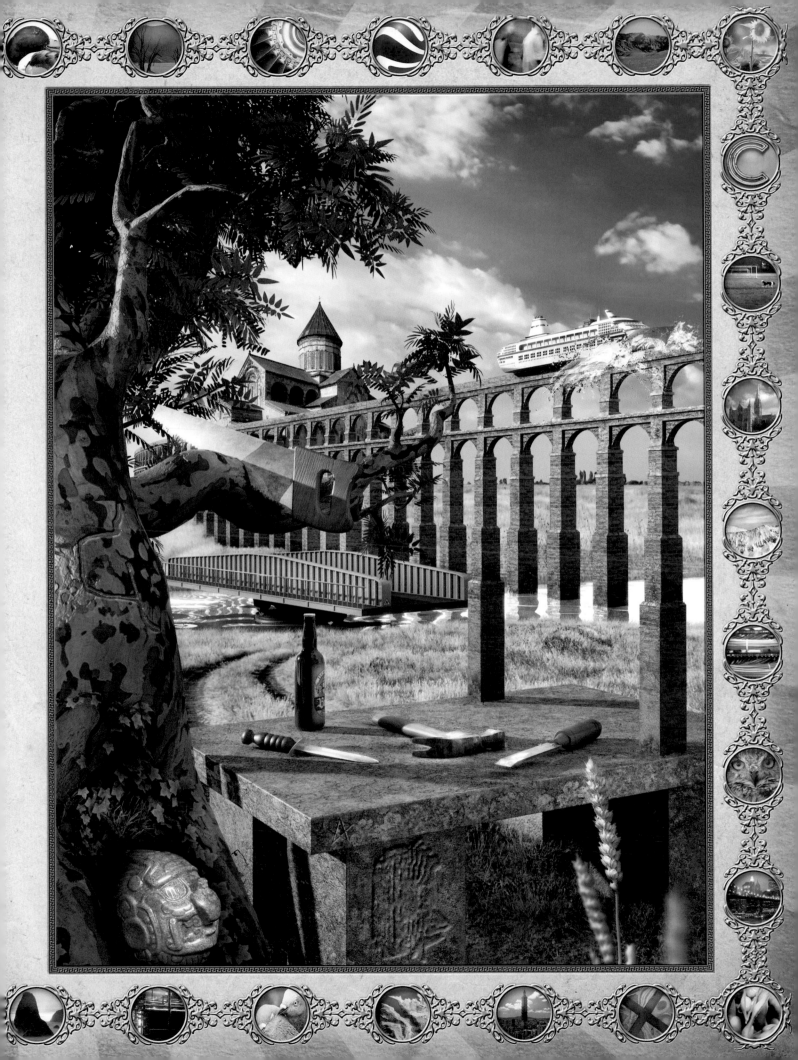

4. JOHN AND THE WILD

Heading southwards, I turn a curious bend and in front of me, the world drops away. Far below, strange black clouds ebb and flow, shattering and reforming as they go. Splintered paths and trails open before me, tempting me onwards, but I am reluctant to surrender myself to their charm and truth. The time will soon be right, but not yet. Not quite.

Instead, I perch on a coppery rock, and survey the lands beneath. Mankind has scattered careless towns across the Earth like jewels, glittering brightly in the sun. This is the perfect spot to admire their beauty, to look them up and down. Get in close, and the view of the whole is lost, exploding into a myriad of unique details. Like all things, they lack the unity that they appear to have from afar. But then, nothing is truly solid; reality is little more than an illusion brought on by the weaknesses of our sight. The thought gives me momentum, if not direction, and I spin off uncertainly.

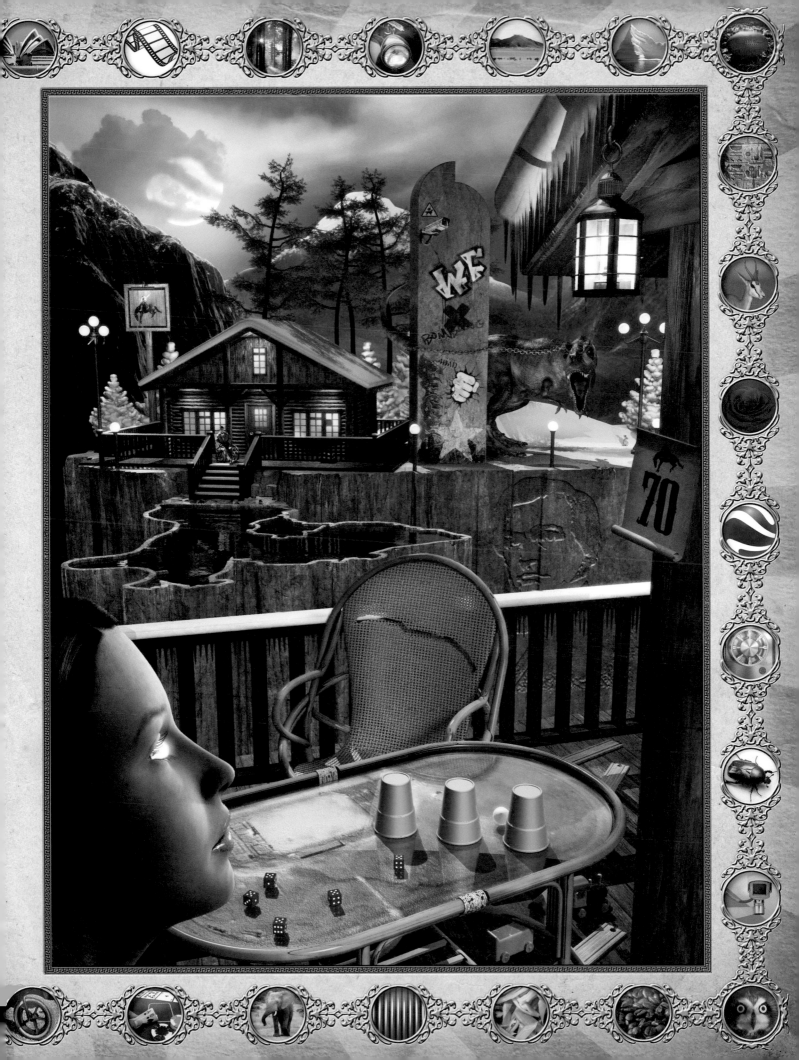

5. THE CAVE MOUTH

6. SCARLET CHAMBERS

Inset into a green and pleasant hillside, a line of rough-hewn entrances beckon to me seductively. Who am I to resist such a delicious call? I make my way to where they lie, and select the fifth of eight. A tunnel awaits me, hospitably cool in the summer warmth, brightened by the light pouring through the crystal veins that seam its walls.

Just shy of two dozen footfalls later, the stone around me opens out, unfolding. There is a haunting scent on the air, familiar yet just out of reach. The cavern before me is a bubble in the rock, glistening brightly. For a fanciful moment, I fear that it might pop. Four paths forge onwards, leading to new worlds and old.

I pick the one that best suits my taste, and laugh, giddy with relief. The light tinges crimson as I enter, perhaps suggesting woes to come, but I press on regardless.

7. SIMPLY ASTOUNDING

Arcane whispers engulf me as I wind downwards. Rock entombs me, its stern caress marking out the borders of my existence. An occasional draught sneaks past, heavy with the smell of incense and spice, and the dark mutterings get louder. In time, I realize that my path is **gently spiralling, coiling in on itself.** I pass a short line of horse-shoe crescents, pointing east, south, west and north, and it seems strange to me that **the coldest and warmest should be adjacent.**

At a junction, an arrow carved into the rock seems to indicate that one path is the more popular; I choose the other. The answers I seek will not lie in the usual places. I progress, and am rewarded with a stretch of checkerboard. I trust that it will lead me towards the truth, and advance boldly. Before long, the glimmer of moonlight informs me that I have chosen wisely. A little while further, and **I realize that I can hear the sea.**

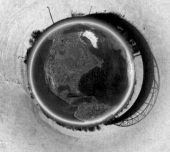

8. IN THE SUN

Stairs bring me to the foot of a mighty church. It rises as a series of increasingly narrow stages, eight becoming four becoming two before finally melding into a delicately rippled spire surmounted by a cross. Persistent arches lead nowhere, or everywhere.

It seems to me that the ghosts of years past flit in and out of the columns, and through the solemn windows. If ever there was a place for haunts and fetches, then surely this is it. A half-dozen ravens rest in the churchyard, studiously avoiding each other's gazes. This truly is a sight to behold.

A peal of bells marks the time, and I find to my surprise that the hour is near at hand. This is not a healthy hour, and I would not be blamed for nothing. I turn my back, and find that an avenue stretches before me. At its end, there is a tacit promise of treasure, of wealth as yet unseen. But the treasure is not mine, and I am having none of it. I turn away entirely, to continue my journey.

51.515446 -0.653015 148 • -37.110757 -12.282455 11830 • 47.082844 -70.921218 828

42.881908 47.656599 165 • 51.271085 -1.844192 117 • 19.409720 -155.749496 106 • -26.294915 -80.111576 715

-105.942749 531 • 34.938802 6.386368 145 • 53.247302 26.048851 1550 • 44.350958 -151.738055 11540 • -16.498919

51.184734 -1.434597 3750 • 50.959908 -0.892367 185 • -34.211098 -56.150946 662

-39.295509 174.061000 19340 • 57.166834 -93.982098 3390 • 32.153346 59.959668 7800

9. DREAMING

Walking through the city of foxes in the half-lit moments before dawn, I find myself approaching a gigantic building, a towering six stories in height.

Eight roads lead towards it,

each running almost up to a set of mighty hazel doors. In the distance, a wanderer approaches, dressed as if for the deep desert. We exchange nods.

I step up to the doors and push.

They swing open silently, and I walk through into a library to rival that of legendary Alexandria itself. A great central chamber, filled with bookcases, offers access to a myriad alcoves, each one in turn promising its own secrets and adventures. I could spend a thousand lifetimes here, and still not learn a thousandth of the wisdom it contains.

I pick a winding path between paper cliffs, increasingly enchanted. Finally, I can go no further, so I settle comfortably. Then I lift up a book, bloated with secrets, and open it. I read, **and am immediately transported...**

49.242661 -108.006968 2460 • 37.419804 -122.082283 23 • -15.734515 -70.358757 6550 • -21.816295 114.165593 2235

54.259561 603 • 46.011659 252 • -111.792734 32.733474 • -164.419402 9950 • 62.855384 33 • 5.115418 52.087486

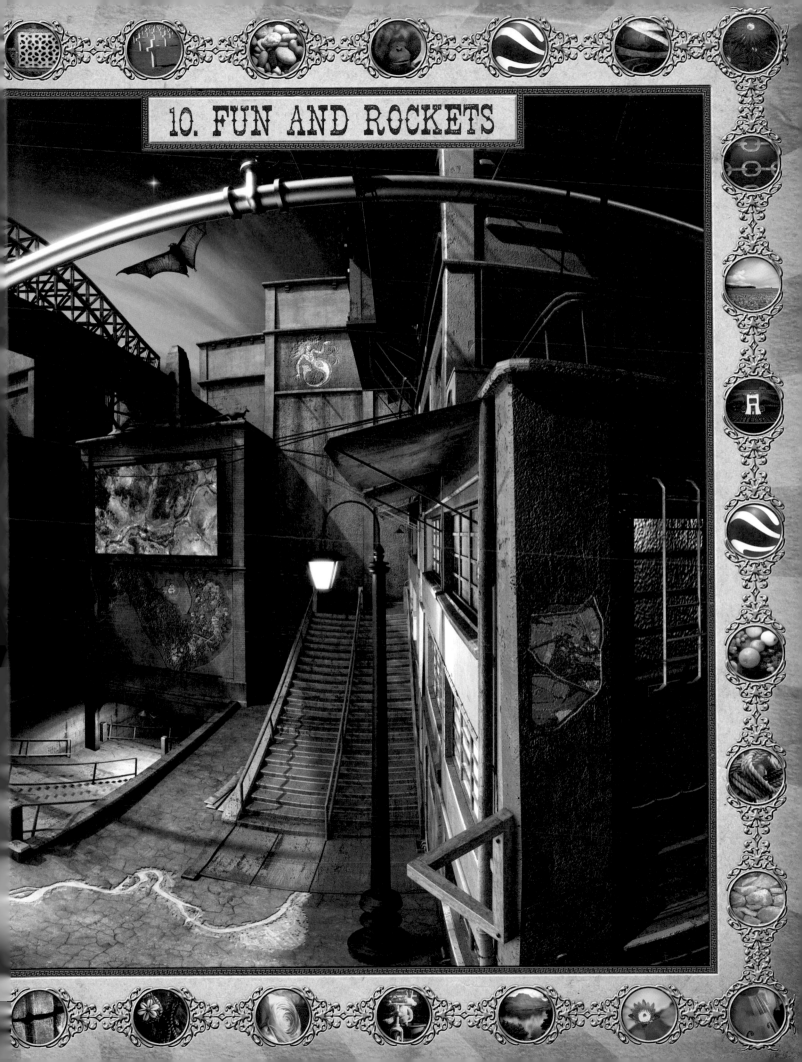

10. FUN AND ROCKETS

11. CHILDREN OF THE WHITE FLOWER

The truth is that there was a time when the **men of the shore cowered in terror** at the thought of the dragons. Filled with dread, they would flee at the merest hint of those ferocious metal teeth and wild eyes, that tough hide and stinking breath. Dragons invariably came from the north, flying over the sea, and they left fire and death in their wake.

Only tumbled stones now remain of their lairs and camps. All else is gone, scattered to the winds, and **the singing mountains no longer** know them. The dark that once arose has fallen again, cast out of this time. Surely that is a sign.

In one such ruin, I discovered a small heap of oranges, stacked carefully. It seemed an oddly acidic cairn, but lacking any apples or nuts, I took one, and devoured it. If I had not done so, I doubt that I would have survived the times to come.

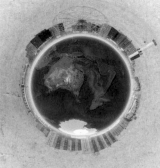

12. BADGERSET

Stars appear to glisten on the chamber ceiling, a mile or more above my head. The streets below are a crazy network of claustrophobic alleys, candle-light glittering through the smoky fug. Perched between the two, I find a rare moment of peace, bringing a measure of calm to my troubled mind's fancies.

This is an uncanny place,

home to bats and weasels and wild, drunken revelling. Somewhere in the spider-web of buildings below, I can hear the orgiastic melodies of crazy musicians. The locals will be yelling and cheering their appreciation, swaying alarmingly in time with the heady beat..

Somewhere out there, persuasive secrets are waiting to be pieced together. Alarming insights can be granted to those with the reckless determination to uncover shadowy truths. It is a dangerous path to tread, but sometimes that is simply the way it has to be. I shall be watchful, and ensure that I do not fall prey to the strange things that lurk in wait.

What gentleman could do less?

13. PARSIMONY

Are you comfortable in your world?
There is much that feels safe and cosy in the familiar.
Turn the lights on, and night-time fears evaporate.
But in my travels, I have learnt the truth; that much
of the reliable daily experience that we bank on
is nothing more than a sweet deception.

Our pleasant reality is a tiny oasis of sanity adrift
on oceans of static madness. Journey as I have,
through rumour and myth and dream, and it
becomes impossible to cling to the tidy dreams
which we mistake for meaning.

In one fevered vision, I saw an island of vast
monoliths and decrepit temples. The stones were
buried in vile mud, and dripped with slime and weed.
They towered above me, and yet
somehow their angles were all wrong. The air
was heavy with the stench of meat. I caught a
glimpse of heavy, ancient doors, and was
roused from my trance by own screams.
I pay the price willingly, but it is heavy.

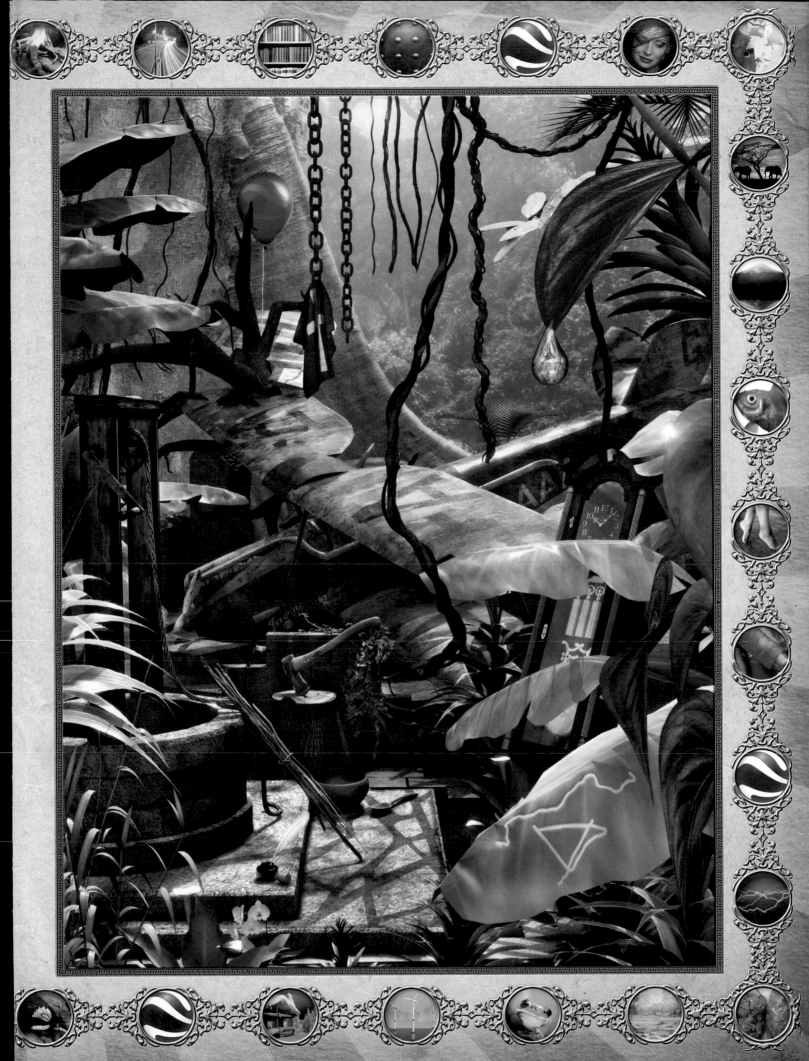

14. GREEN MAN

Right is not a virtue that can be bought. To be upstanding, you must be true. Often, rectitude must serve as its own reward, for this is not a virtuous world. For the wise however, such acts are to be prized more highly than pearls. This is the lesson of Solomon: try however you may to fill the void, it is only the balm of decency that offers peace and satisfaction.

As my journey comes to its inevitable close, **I find that the truth is clear.** All voyages start and end in the same place - home, however you choose to define it. I have taken several grave steps in my quest, and learnt things that I could never have guessed. Now that I find myself **approaching the end of my travels,** and I return to the beginning, I discover that I am greatly enriched. I have become the master, and discovered that this means I will always be the student. But now, everything I need to know lies within my grasp.

I have looked into the labyrinth, and seen **myself staring back out at me.**

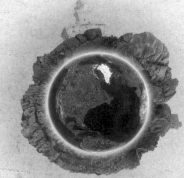

THE GREAT GLOBAL
TREASURE HUNT

ON GOOGLE EARTH

Entry to this competition is via the website

www.jointhetreasurehunt.com

using clues contained in this book, however, no purchase of this
book is necessary to enter. The competition opens at 11:59pm GMT
on 1 September 2011 and closes at midnight GMT March 31, 2012.
The prize is € 50,000 (fifty thousand euro) cash.

THIS IS A CARLTON BOOK
Published in Great Britain in 2011 by
Carlton Books Limited, 20 Mortimer Street, London W1T 3JW

Google Earth is a trademark of Google Inc.

A CIP catalogue for this book is available from the British Library.

ISBN 978-1-84732-623-2

Printed in Dubai
10 9 8 7 6 5 4 3 2 1

Editorial Director: Piers Murray Hill
Editorial Manager: Roland Hall
Design Director: Russell Porter
Picture Research: Steve Behan
Production: Claire Halligan

All photographs supplied by Istockphoto.com with the exception of the
following: (cathedral) Corbis/Arcaid/Richard Bryant; (jade head) 2010
Tony Rath/Tony Rath Photography/tonyrath.com, image courtesy of
NICH – Institute of Archaeology; elk (courtesy of the Harris Museum &
Art Gallery); (cotton mill) Topfoto.co.uk
Every effort has been made to acknowledge correctly and contact
the source and/or copyright holder of each picture and Carlton Books
Limited apologises for any unintentional errors or omissions which will
be corrected in future editions of this book.